577

FORESTS FOR LIFE

Edward Parker

WAYLAND

In association with WorldWide Fund For Nature and Forests For Life campaign

PROTECTING OUR PLANET

 FORESTS FOR LIFE

 FUELS FOR THE FUTURE

 KEEPING THE AIR CLEAN

 KEEPING WATER CLEAN

 PROTECTING WILD PLACES

 WASTE, RECYCLING AND RE-USE

Produced for Wayland (Publishers) Limited by
Roger Coote Publishing
Gissing's Farm, Fressingfield
Eye, Suffolk IP21 5SH, England

Designer: Tim Mayer

First published in 1997 by
Wayland (Publishers) Limited
61 Western Road, Hove
East Sussex BN3 1JD, England

Find Wayland on the internet at http://www.wayland.co.uk

Cataloguing in Publication Data
Forests for the future. – (Protecting our planet)
    1.Forests and forestry – Juvenile literature
    2.Forest conservation – Juvenile literature
    333.7'5

ISBN 07502 2004 X

Printed and bound in Italy by L.E.G.O. S.p.A., Vicenza

CONTENTS

INTRODUCTION

Forests form some of the most spectacular and important ecosystems on earth, providing habitats for millions of animal and plant species. They are also home to millions of indigenous people around the world who depend on them directly for food, shelter, fuel and medicines.

We do not, however, need to live in or near the world's great forests to benefit from them. Almost every aspect of our daily lives, even in cities, is linked to forests. The oxygen we breathe is regulated by forests. The water we drink is recycled by trees, and tropical rain forests help maintain our global climate. Many of our most popular foods such as chocolate, bananas and coffee originated in forests. Even fish fingers are held together using wood pulp from trees!

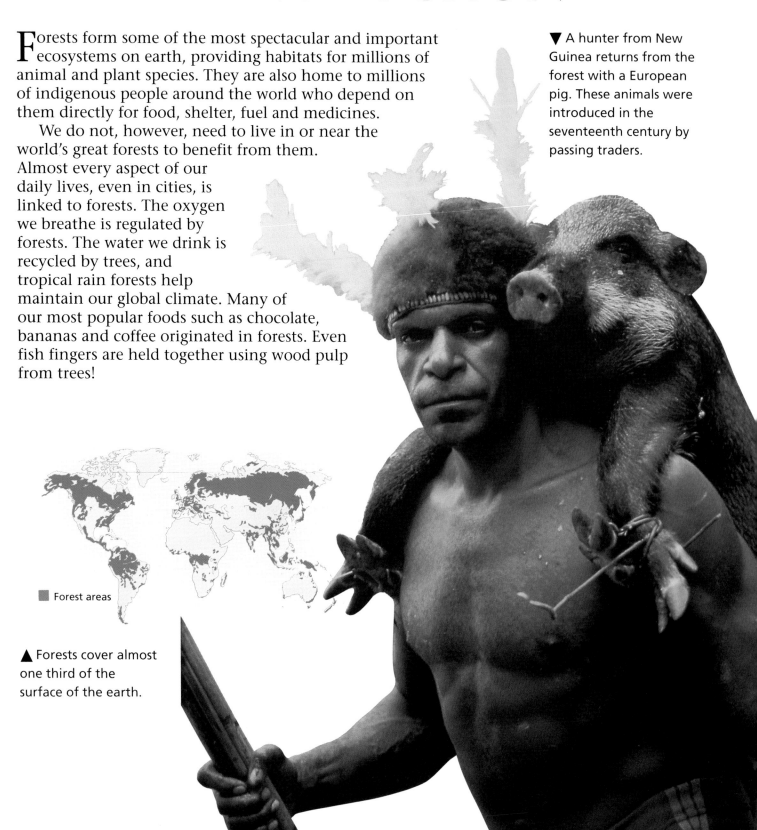

▼ A hunter from New Guinea returns from the forest with a European pig. These animals were introduced in the seventeenth century by passing traders.

■ Forest areas

▲ Forests cover almost one third of the surface of the earth.

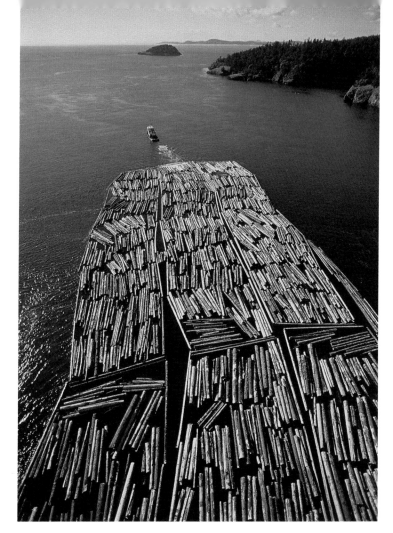
▲ A tug pulls a huge floating boom of logs to a saw mill in Skagit Bay, Washington State, USA.

Forests have provided essential resources for the great civilizations of the past. Today, they provide the industrial world with many of the raw materials needed for multi-billion dollar industries. These materials include timber, wood pulp, gums, resins, nuts, fruits and medicinal plants. Products from trees are used for a huge range of consumer goods from cancer drugs to spectacle frames, aircraft tyres and car paints. Every time we read a book or magazine, or take a picture using photographic film, we use wood pulp from forest trees.

Forests cover around 30 per cent of the earth's land surface. They are centres of great biological richness, containing more than 70 per cent of the world's land-living plant and animal species. But they are disappearing at an alarming rate. Large areas of tropical rain forest have already been cut down, and much of the ancient temperate rain forest in North America and Chile is due to be clear-felled in the next ten years. Forests are vital to life on earth and they are a resource that must be managed wisely.

TREE FACTS

The oldest living organism on earth today is the bristle cone pine which can live for more than 5,000 years. This is equivalent to 200 human generations.

● Californian redwood trees can weigh up to 6,000 tonnes, making them the largest living organisms on the planet.

● Some of the trees in temperate forests of north-west America can grow to over 100 m tall, and are the biggest living organisms alive today. Even bigger were the monkey thorn trees of South Africa's Transvaal. They reached a staggering 120 m tall and 45 m around the trunk, but they had all been cut down by the beginning of this century.

● A 200-year-old arctic willow may have a trunk only about as thick as a human finger.

THE WORLD'S FORESTS

Trees have existed on the earth for around 275 million years, and for 90 million years they dominated the earth's vegetation. During this period – known as the Carboniferous Era – millions of tonnes of plant material were laid down and later compressed under sediments over very long periods of time, to form the fossil fuels such as coal, oil and gas that we depend on today.

During their long history many types of tree and forest have evolved. Today there are thousands of different tree species growing in a great variety of forest types – from tropical rain forests and coastal mangrove forests to the pine forests of the sub Arctic.

HUMAN INFLUENCE

Forests throughout the world have been changed by people. Where a forest has been relatively undisturbed by human activity it is called **primary** forest. Where people have had a significant effect and the original forest has been greatly altered this is known as **secondary** forest. A **plantation** is an artificial forest where tree species have been planted to provide a particular product, such as timber.

▶ Temperate pine forests in Baker National Park, Washington State, USA.

Trees can be divided into two broad types: conifers and broadleaved trees. Conifer means literally 'cone bearing' and these trees are typically evergreen and often have needle-shaped leaves. Broadleaved trees are often deciduous (losing their leaves seasonally) and have a wide variety of leaf shapes.

The world's forests are generally divided into three main types. These are: boreal or northern forests, temperate forests and tropical forests. However, there is not usually any clear line to show where one forest type ends and another begins. The situation is also complicated by altitude, since highland areas in temperate or tropical forests can contain trees that are usually only found in much cooler locations.

▲ The most common types of forest in the shaded areas.

Boreal forest
Temperate forest
Tropical forest

BOREAL FORESTS

The boreal forests stretch across Russia, Norway, Finland, Sweden, USA and Canada, forming an almost continuous belt around the earth. Although they are generally found between the latitudes 45–60° North, some Siberian forests are situated as far north as 70°. Together, these forests make up one of the world's last great wildernesses which, until recently, had been little altered by human activity.

Boreal forests are characterized by hot summers, extremely cold winters and low rainfall. The result of this harsh climate is a growing season of only three months each year, which is too short for most types of trees. Only hardy conifers such as spruce, larch, fir and pine trees thrive in these conditions, although it can take a tree 150–200 years to reach maturity.

▲ Boreal forests consist mainly of slow-growing needleleaf trees such as larch.

TEMPERATE FORESTS

There are many types of temperate forest and they occur in both the northern and southern hemispheres. The word 'temperate' means moderate and this describes the weather conditions that are found in the parts of the world where these forests grow with warm summers, mild winters and high rainfall, spread evenly throughout the year. These conditions are ideal for both conifers and broadleaved trees.

Temperate rain forest grows along the north-west coast of North America. Although it is dominated by conifer tree species, such as Sitka spruce and Douglas fir, it is quite unlike the conifer forests of the boreal region. North America's temperate rain forests are home to some of the oldest and largest trees on earth. Douglas fir trees, for example, can be up to 90 m high and 5 m in diameter.

In other temperate areas, forests are generally made up of a mixture of broadleaved trees and conifers. In Britain, for example, forests and woodlands range from those dominated by oak and beech in the lowlands, to birch and pine forests in the uplands.

▲ Temperate forests consist of a complex mix of needleleaf (left) and broadleaf trees (right) including the largest species, such as Hemlock and Giant Redwood.

▼ Mosses thrive on living and dead trees in the moist and mild climate of a temperate rain forest.

▲ Around half the world's tropical forests are dry like this one in the north-western Transvaal, South Africa.

TROPICAL FORESTS

Located between the tropics of Cancer and Capricorn, tropical forests cover approximately 14 per cent of the earth's land surface. There are two main types: tropical rain forests and tropical dry forests.

Tropical rain forests are the most complex and diverse ecosystems on earth and scientists have estimated that they could contain between 50 and 90 per cent of the world's plant and animal species. For example, in one 50-hectare plot of tropical rain forest in Malaysia 835 tree species have been identified.

Tropical rain forests are found in hot and humid conditions, where the average temperature during the coldest month of the year is no lower than 18° C and there is at least 100 mm of rain every month.

In contrast to the dense, luxuriant tropical rain forest, tropical dry forests often have trees that are widely scattered and are usually small and scrubby in appearance. They tend to grow in areas where the climate is hot and dry, and the trees may lose their leaves during the driest months. Whilst these dry forests do not contain as many species as rain forests, they are the habitat for some of the world's most magnificent animals such as elephants, rhinos and lions.

▲ Tropical forests tend to contain a wide variety of broadleaf evergreen trees like the one shown here.

FORESTS AND THE WORLD ENVIRONMENT

Forests are valuable for many reasons. The timber, foods and medicines that use ingredients from forests are worth billions of dollars every year. However, they are also extremely valuable to us in ways that are difficult to calculate in terms of money.

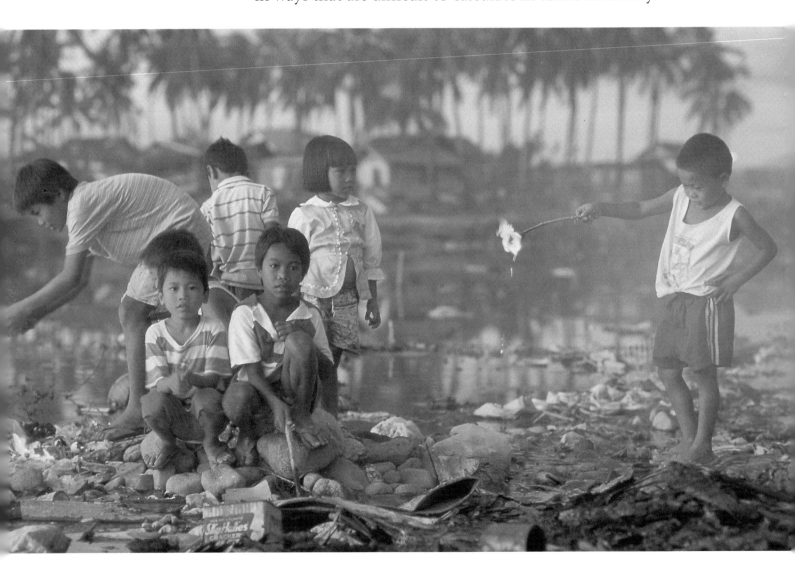

These children in the Philippines were made homeless and orphans by flash floods. This happened because the forests on surrounding hills had been cut down, increasing the amount of water flowing down hillsides.

FLOODS AND DROUGHT

Trees play an extremely important role in the control of floods and droughts. During torrential rains the leaves in the forest canopy break the fall of rain drops, reducing their impact on the soil and young plants below. The spaces in the soil made by tree roots then help the water to soak in. Forests work like huge sponges soaking up rainfall and releasing it slowly throughout the year into streams and topping up underground water supplies.

Land covered with trees and other plants absorbs 20 times as much rain water as bare earth. Where forests have been removed, the rain water flows over the surface of the land causing floods. And because only a small proportion of the rain water soaks into the ground there is often too little left for the rest of the year.

▲ Rain falling over the rain-forested foothills of the Bolivian Andes.

A PHILIPPINE DISASTER

In November 1991 flash floods raced down the hillsides above the coastal town of Ormoc in the Philippines. Within minutes the water rose to 4 m deep in the streets. Seven thousand people were drowned.

The tragedy was blamed on illegal logging, which had stripped the hills of the dense rain forest that once clothed them. Without the forests to absorb it, the torrential tropical rain raced down valleys, smashing houses and bursting river banks. Thousands of illegaly cut logs were swept down from the mountain-sides, giving a clue to the cause of the disaster.

Ninety years ago 80 per cent of the Philippines was covered in forest. Now it has fewer trees per person than any other Southeast Asian country, mostly because of illegal logging.

PHILIPPINES

Manila •

• Ormoc

India is a good example of how the cutting down of forests causes floods and droughts. About 60 million hectares of land in India are now vulnerable to flooding: more than twice as much as 30 years ago. And in the Indian state of Uttar Pradesh alone – where there has been heavy logging activity – the number of villages that are short of water has risen from 17,000 to 70,000 in the last twenty years.

▼ This diagram shows the effects of deforestation. Tree loss leads to soil erosion and landslides. These are often followed by the silting-up of rivers and reservoirs, which shortens the life of dams and causes flooding.

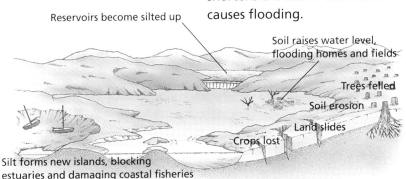

Reservoirs become silted up

Soil raises water level, flooding homes and fields

Trees felled

Soil erosion

Land slides

Crops lost

Silt forms new islands, blocking estuaries and damaging coastal fisheries

WILDLIFE AND BIODIVERSITY

Forests in all their forms provide habitats for more than 70 per cent of all land-living species on the planet. The rain forests provide the most dramatic example of this, containing over half of all terrestrial species but covering only 6 per cent of the earth's land surface. In a typical 1,000-hectare patch of rain forest, biologists would expect to find 1,500 species of flowering plant, 750 kinds of trees, 400 bird species and more than 150 kinds of butterflies. A forest on one volcano in the Philippines has more plant species than the entire USA! Forests even influence sea life – 70 per cent of all fish caught throughout the world hatch in coastal mangroves and estuaries.

A pig-tailed macaque in the forests of Borneo.

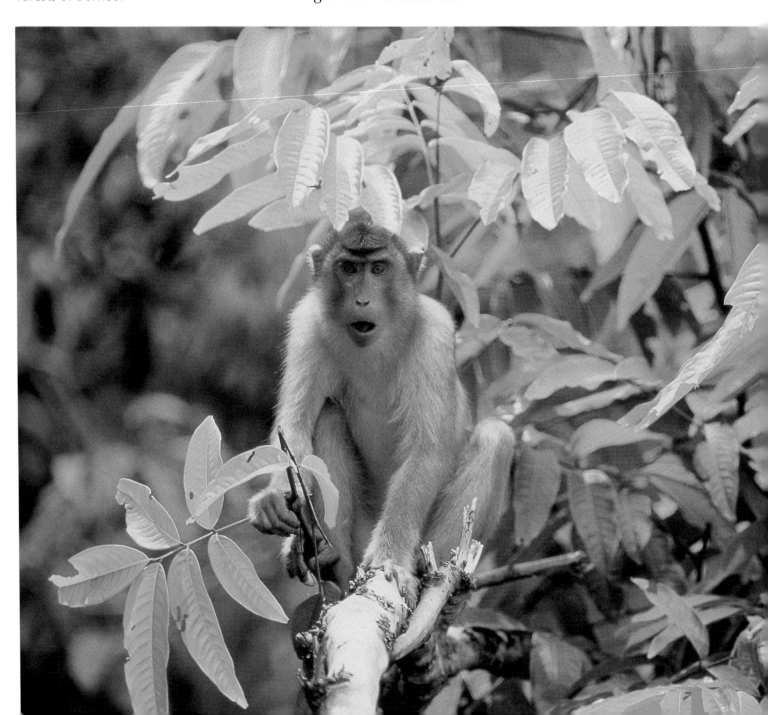

MANGROVES – FORESTS WITH THEIR FEET IN THE SEA

Mangroves are a special type of rain forest that line one-quarter of the world's tropical coastlines. The 55 different types of mangrove cover an area of approximately 2,400 square kilometres.

The trees are readily identifiable because of their bell-shaped root system that lifts the trunk above the mud and water. These 'breathing' roots enable mangroves to survive in areas of very salty water, usually along coastlines, or in water with reduced oxygen, for example in swamps.

Mangrove forests give coastlines vital protection from the destructive effects of storm-force winds and waves. They also provide a sheltered environment and the clean, silt-free water that thousands of aquatic species need to breed in. More than 2,000 species of fish and invertebrates (for example, shrimps) are believed to use mangroves as spawning grounds.

Mangroves provide important resources for people who live along tropical coasts. These forests have been shown to be as productive as farmlands, providing shellfish, shrimps, crabs, fish and firewood for millions of people around the world.

▲ Many ocean fish and crustaceans breed in the mangrove forest because they can find protection from predators among the roots of the trees.

■ Mangroves

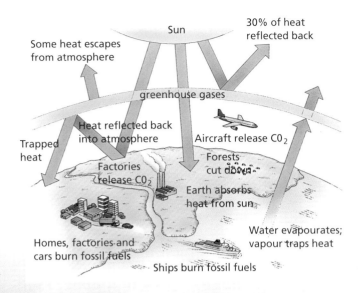

Sun

30% of heat reflected back

Some heat escapes from atmosphere

greenhouse gases

Heat reflected back into atmosphere

Aircraft release CO_2

Trapped heat

Factories release CO_2

Forests cut down

Earth absorbs heat from sun

Homes, factories and cars burn fossil fuels

Water evapourates; vapour traps heat

Ships burn fossil fuels

▼ Forests absorb the energy from the sun by transpiring - releasing water vapour through pores in the leaves. This helps make the local climate in tropical forest areas cooler.

GLOBAL WARMING

Scientific evidence has recently shown that the earth is warming up. This has been caused mainly by an increase in the proportion of carbon dioxide gas in the atmosphere. Presently, carbon dioxide in the atmosphere rises by 1 per cent each year. If this trend continues, the world will experience a temperature rise of 3° C by the year 2100, making the earth warmer than at any time during the last 100,000 years. To give an idea of how serious this is, a rise of 4° C would mean that the earth would be exposed to temperatures not experienced since 40 million years ago.

As trees grow they absorb carbon dioxide from the air. Together the world's trees and soils contain two billion tonnes of carbon. This is locked up in complex chemicals, such as fats and proteins, found in living and dead organic material. However, when organic matter, such as wood, decomposes or is burnt it releases most of its stored carbon into the atmosphere as carbon dioxide gas. Cutting down forests has produced half of all man-made emissions over last 130 years. The other half has come from burning fossil fuels such as coal, oil and gas, which are the compressed remains of plants that grew millions of years ago.

Scientists have proposed planting trees as a way of collecting and storing carbon to help counteract the build up of carbon dioxide. Their research has shown that while fast-growing plantation trees could help, protecting 'old growth' forests is a much more efficient way of storing carbon. Each year 16 per cent of atmospheric carbon dioxide is cycled through plants, and forests contain up to 85 per cent of all carbon that is bound up in living organisms.

CLIMATE

The weather in forested regions is generally milder, moister and less variable than in treeless regions. The boreal forests, for example, warm the sub-Arctic region by providing a dark mass capable of absorbing heat from the sun. Trees in hot areas, on the other hand, have a cooling effect.

Forests also affect the amount of rain that falls on them. Trees pump up vast quantities of water from the ground. This water evaporates from the leaves, releasing moisture into the air. The moisture gathers as clouds and then falls as rain again. At least half of the rain that falls on the Amazon is recycled in this way.

Where the rain forest has been cut down in Madagascar large quantities of soil have been washed away, sometimes leaving just bare rock.

SOIL LOSS

Trees catch much of the rain falling on to a forest, softening its destructive power before it reaches the ground. Tree roots create spaces for the water to soak away through and help to bind the soil. When trees are removed, especially from mountain-sides, the soil is soon washed away by rain. A recent study in Côte D'Ivoire has shown that a deforested hill loses 500 times as much soil as one covered with trees. Forest destruction around the world causes the loss of 50 billion tonnes of topsoil every year.

Soil erosion is now so severe that it can be seen from space. Astronauts have commented that the African island of Madagascar looks as if it is bleeding to death because of the millions of tonnes of red topsoil washed into the Indian Ocean from the deforested hillsides.

FORESTS AND HUMAN LIFE

Wooden houses being built in New Zealand. They are safer in areas where there is threat of earthquakes because the frames are more flexible than steel and concrete.

Forests have been vitally important to humans throughout our history. In many religions the origins of our prehistoric ancestors are linked to trees and the importance of forests and trees themselves lives on in ancient customs. Belief in a 'Tree of Life' which links heaven, earth and the underworld is a very ancient one and this symbol appears in myths from the Arctic to Australia.

Throughout history people have relied on trees for fuel, tools and building materials. The societies of Mycenae and Minoan Crete – which existed between 4,500 and 3,200 year ago – used 120 pine trees to smelt every ingot of bronze. However, in the fourth century BC the Greek philosopher Plato was already writing about the deforested hills around Athens, noting that 'what now remains is like the skeleton of a sick man'. After cutting down most of the forests near Rome the Romans were forced to expand their empire in order to secure vital supplies of wood.

War had a particularly severe effect on the forests of Europe in the Middle Ages and later. For example, more than a quarter of a million trees were cut down to build the Christian and Turkish fleets that fought at the Battle of Lepanto in 1571. By the eighteenth century, it took 2,000 large trees to make a single warship.

▲ A painting depicting the wooden galleons of the Spanish Armada at sea.

The Industrial Revolution, which began in Europe around the mid-eighteenth century, was powered by coal – the fossilized remains of trees that died millions of years ago.

FOREST PEOPLE

More than 140 million people live in or around forests and rely directly on them. For example, half the world's population uses wood as a fuel for cooking and/or heating. Whilst an increasing proportion of the people who now live in forests are relative new-comers, around 1–2.5 million indigenous people have been living in them for many thousands of years. For these people forests have traditionally provided everything including, their spiritual and cultural identity.

Indigenous people have developed a great understanding of the nature of the forests in which they live. Many know of practical uses for almost all of the trees in their traditional areas – for foods, medicines, hunting, fishing or building materials or for their spiritual needs.

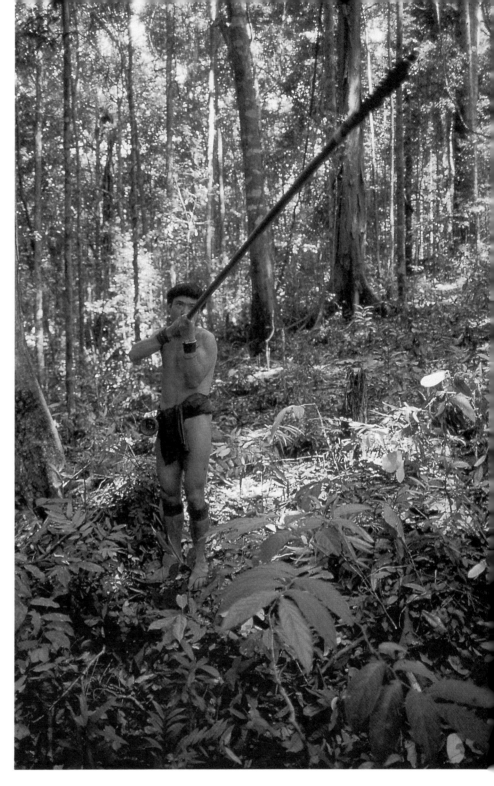

▲ A Penan man from the rain forest hunting with a hardwood blow pipe, on the island of Sarawak, Malaysia.

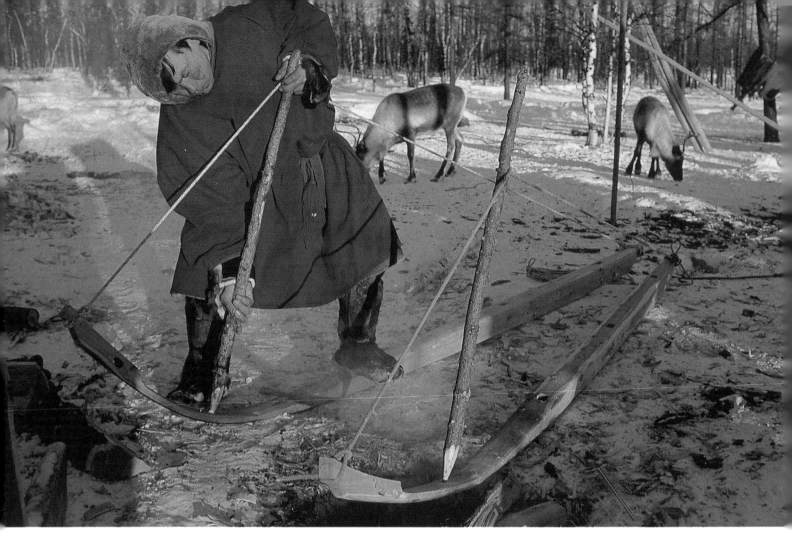

A Nenets reindeer herder bends the larch runners of a new sled into shape.

Arctic Ocean

• Naryanmar

• Syktyvkar

Salekhard •

Dudinka
•
• Norilsk

☐ Nenets

RUSSIA

Arctic Circle

• Khanty Mansiysk

0 100 200 300 400 miles

0   200   400   600 km

A NENETS MAKES A SLED

One of the native peoples in northern Siberia are a group of reindeer herders known as the Nenets. Each spring they migrate 1,000 kilometres with their reindeer herds to the summer pastures in the north of the Yamal Peninsula. They head south each Autumn to over-winter in the forests just south of the Arctic Circle. Each group of herders is made up of several families and up to 4,000 reindeer.

The Nenets make their sleds in a way that has changed little over the last thousand years. They use larch wood from the Siberian forest known as the taiga. It takes several days to make each sled, which usually requires wood from three larch trees. The runners are made by steaming and gently bending them into shape over heat. The whole construction is held together by wooden pegs.

Indigenous people don't only live in tropical rain forests but in many other forest areas around the world. For example, the temperate rain forests of Alaska are the ancestral home of the Tlinglit and other traditional peoples; Aborigine groups live in the forests of northern Australia; while the Mahgreb are Berber people who live in the Atlas mountains of Tunisia, where North Africa's last forest reserves are found. The fact that some of the world's most diverse and least damaged forests are also the homes of indigenous peoples is no accident: the people have utilized but protected them for thousands of years. Many of these areas have recently been seen by others as prime areas to turn into parks or nature reserves. After decades of mostly appalling treatment by outsiders, many indigenous peoples are outraged by this view. They are demanding that their land rights be observed and that they be allowed to control their own lands.

Forests around the world provide a livelihood for many forest people who are not indigenous to them. In Brazil, rubber tappers and Brazil nut gatherers gain employment from the forest. In Asia and Africa the harvesting of rattan (a climbing palm) provides jobs for tens of thousands of people.

Collecting and cracking open Brazil nuts provides thousands of jobs in the Amazon without destroying the rain forest.

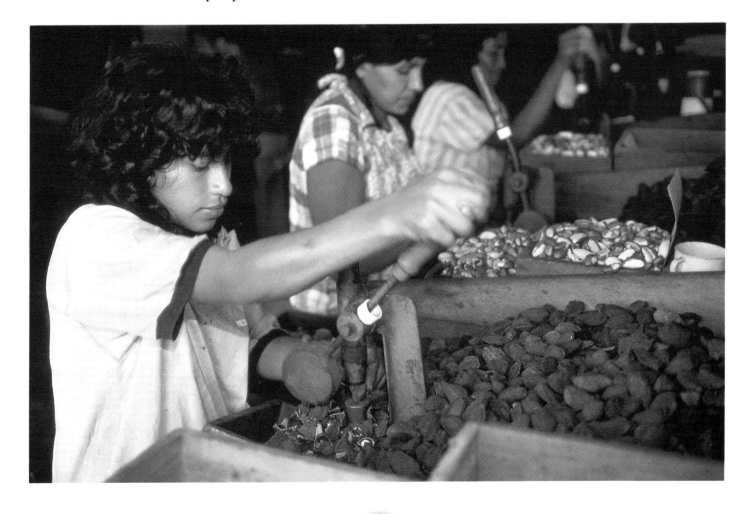

CELLULOSE – BUILDING BLOCKS OF PLANTS AND INDUSTRY

Cellulose is one of the most valuable products derived from trees. After processing it is powdered and dried and is used as the raw material for many industrial products. These include paper, viscose (a man-made fibre used to make clothing), acetate and triacetate. Some of the final products made from cellulose include photographic film, spectacle frames, combs, nappies, toothbrushes, knitting needles and even car steering wheels. Cellulose is also used a thickener and binder in products such as paints and toothpaste, and in foods such as fish fingers where it helps to keep the batter from disintegrating.

Paper is the most important product made with cellulose from trees.
It currently accounts for 12 per cent of all the timber used in the world.

China 20,757,000
Canada 16,900,000
Germany 12,998,000
Finland 9,304,000
Sweden 8,503,000
Japan 28,380,000
Others
USA 75,045,000

PAPER PRODUCTION 1991-93
(Cubic Metres)

World Production 247,320,000

A high-tech Finnish paper mill designed to minimise pollution. In 1993 over 253 million tonnes of paper were made world-wide.

NON-TIMBER FOREST PRODUCTS

Forests are often given a value in terms of the timber they can produce but wood is only one of many forest products. The range of non-timber forest products is truly vast and includes foods, fibres, building materials, fuel, medicinal and aromatic plants, gums and latexes. Forest peoples around the world have used their forests' resources for countless practical purposes – from beautiful clothing made from bark to powerful medicines to cure fevers. And it is the knowledge of forest peoples that has been used in many cases to develop modern consumer goods and medicines.

Rattans – a group of climbing palms – are an example of this. Rattan canes have been used for thousands of years used by the peoples of Southeast Asia. Today, furniture and other items made from rattans are worth more than US $8 billion every year. Spices like cinnamon and cardamom are also very valuable forest products – now worth over US $1 billion annually – that were first used by native peoples. Many of the most expensive perfumes in the world contain ingredients from tropical forest plants, while most of the cheaper scents are made by reacting resin from temperate pine trees with chemicals. Plant products from forests are used in almost every area of our lives. While most of us have chewed gum containing chicle, a sap which is collected from Central American rain forest trees, professional golfers use balls covered in balata latex, another sap which is tapped from the forests of Guyana and Surinam.

Cane furniture made from rattan being taken to market in Thailand.

21

A healing man on Sumba Island in Indonesia uses a forest root called manupeu to treat an ill person.

FORESTS AND WORLD HEALTH

Forests are very important to health. Up to 80 per cent of the world's population still rely on traditional medicines, and the ingredients for many of these come directly from trees or plants that grow in forests.

The ancient system of herbal medicine practised in India, Sri Lanka and Southeast Asia – known as Ayurveda – uses over 8,000 plant remedies, while traditional Chinese doctors use about 5,000 species of plant. Many of these are found in forests. Indigenous peoples have developed very specialized knowledge of the uses of forest plants. The Kayapo Indians of Brazil, for example, can diagnose and treat over 150 different types of dysentery and diarrhoea alone.

But it is not just traditional doctors who use the forests. The active ingredients in many modern medicines are taken directly from forest plants or trees, while others are made in laboratories by copying the chemical structures they contain. A quarter of all the drugs available on prescription today are extracted directly from plants.

Many plant-based drugs are now used to treat illnesses that were once thought incurable. The rosy periwinkle from Madagascar and the Caribbean has given us two important drugs which help fight forms of cancer. The use of one of these, vincristine, means that four out of every five children who get leukaemia now recover. Active ingredients in the monsoon forest plant known as snake root, or rauvolfia, are very important in controlling high blood pressure and have a tranquilizing effect. An ingredient of the famous Amazonian arrow-poison, curare, is now widely used by surgeons as a muscle-relaxant.

▲ A researcher checks the dried branches of the Pacific Yew. The chemical, taxol, extracted from this tree has been shown to be effective against various types of cancer.

QUININE AND MALARIA

Quinine – one of the world's most precious medicines – comes from the bark of the cinchona tree, a small, attractive, evergreen with glossy leaves and fragrant flowers. South American Indians first used this bark to treat fevers, and they shared this knowledge with Jesuit missionaries working in Peru nearly 400 years ago. In 1633 Father Calancha, a Jesuit priest, wrote of the 'miraculous cures' achieved by drinking a potion made from the powdered bark.

Today, more than 100 million people suffer from the disease malaria, and many of them are treated with quinine. The parasites that cause the disease have become resistant to some of the man-made drugs used to treat it, and quinine is still the most important cure.

When the British ruled India, Europeans who lived there were advised to take quinine in water, as protection against malaria. Flavourings were soon added to improve the bitter taste and the drink became popular. Today, 60 per cent of quinine is used medicinally, the other 40 per cent is used in the drinks industry in tonic water and other drinks.

A nurse in the children's ward of the malaria hospital in Douala, Cameroon, checks the drip connected to an ill child.

Although many pharmaceutical companies are now keen to find new active substances in plants, less than 5 per cent of the world's rain forest species have been studied so far for their value to medicine.

Forests can help us to recover from illness and to relax. Recent studies have shown that hospital patients with a view of trees from their windows recover more quickly than those who can only see other buildings. Forests are important as recreation areas as well.

DISAPPEARING FORESTS

A forest plot is cleared in Zaire by cutting the rain forest trees down and then burning the undergrowth. This type of forest clearance is often referred to as 'slash and burn' agriculture.

Ten thousand years ago forests covered roughly half the land surface on earth. Today, more than 2 billion hectares of this forested area have disappeared. Of the remaining 6.2 billion ha, 1.5 billion hectares of forest are still undisturbed, and are found largely in remote places like northern Canada and Siberia, and the Congo and Amazon river basins.

Although people have been clearing forests throughout history, creating areas that have since become barren or desert, most of the damage to forests has occurred in the last 50 years. Half of the world's tropical rain forests have been destroyed during the twentieth century. In Central America 90 per cent of the rain forest has been destroyed, while only 70,000 square kilometres – or 5 per cent – of India's original forest cover of more than 1.5 million square kilometres now remains.

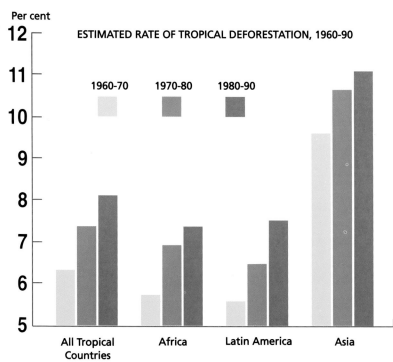

THE CAUSES OF DEFORESTATION

The main causes of forest destruction are:

- Logging for timber
- The movement of people into new areas of forest
- The conversion of forests to land for agriculture, ranching or plantations
- Fuel-wood collection
- Atmospheric pollution.

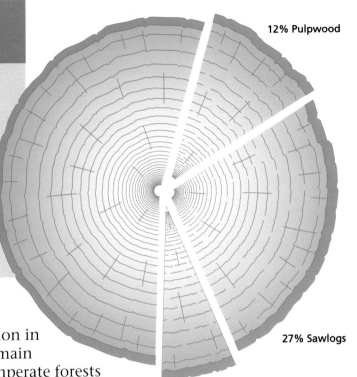

12% Pulpwood

54% Fuelwood

27% Sawlogs

7% Other Industrial

Large-scale farming and cattle ranching are estimated to be the main causes of forest destruction in Latin America, while uncontrolled logging is the main culprit in Asia and Africa. Many of the world's temperate forests are also being destroyed through logging.

JAPAN'S EFFECT ON WORLD FORESTS

Japan is unusual in the world today since nearly three-quarters of its land is covered with pine, cedar or beech forests, many of which are now in protected areas. Japan is one of only a few countries in the world where forest cover is actually increasing. Yet this one country imports more tropical timber than the rest of the world combined.

In the 1960s the Philippines was the main supplier of timber to Japan. Now, most Philippine forests are exhausted. A similar situation arose in Indonesia in the 1970s. By the end of the 1980s Japan had turned its attention elsewhere and 96 per cent of its log imports were coming from Malaysia and Papua New Guinea. In the late 1990s Japan looked further afield for its timber, to countries like Brazil and Chile. Indonesian and Korean companies are also buying up large areas of Amazon rain forest.

Pine logs being loaded on to a ship in Miyako town, Japan. Japanese forests provide only a tiny proportion of the timber used in Japan: most is imported.

Nobody is really sure how much forest still remains in the world, but it is thought that forests are being lost at a rate of 400,000 hectares every day. Despite the public outcry in recent years over the destruction of the Amazon rain forest, and the pledging in 1990 of more than US $500 million by the richest countries of the world to try and save it, Brazilian government figures show that the annual rate of destruction has increased by 34 per cent since 1992. A survey carried out by the United Nations Food and Agriculture Organization showed that the rate of global deforestation has doubled since 1980; by 2025 no large areas of tropical forest will be left, apart from those in a few remote parts of Amazonia, Zaire and Papua New Guinea. Sarawak is currently being deforested faster than anywhere else on earth, to supply timber to the Far East. The Solomon Islands are also allowing Asian logging companies to clear fell most of islands' forests so fast that they will probably all be gone by about 2006.

The demand for tropical timber has risen 16 times over the last 40 years, but it is the USA, Canada and the countries of the former Soviet Union that now provide more than half the world's industrial timber. In both tropical and temperate forests over-logging is not only ruining unique ecosystems and many peoples lives, but threatening the future of the timber industry as well. The World Bank estimates that of the 33 countries that export tropical timber today, only 10 will be still in business beyond the year 2000. China, which is now logging the forests of Tibet, is expected to run out of harvestable forests around 2006.

▶ Logging in the Pacific North-west region of North America. President Collor of Brazil recently pointed out that deforestation occurring in the temperate rain forests of USA and Canada is just as serious as that occurring in the Amazon.

**Map labels:**

■ Remaining forests
□ Deforested areas

VENEZUELA
GUYANA
SURINAM
COLOMBIA
FRENCH GUIANA
Guri Dam
ECUADOR
Balbina Dam
PERU
BRAZIL
BOLIVIA
PARAGUAY
CHILE
ARGENTINA

WASTING WOOD

In many cases forests are destroyed and no use is made of the timber at all. Hydro-electric projects such as the Guri Dam in Venezuela, led to the flooding of 4,000 square kilometres of unique rain forest. The Balbina dam in the heart of the Brazilian Amazon caused the flooding of 400,000 hectares of forest. In projects like these useful timber worth millions of dollars was wasted. Cattle ranchers have also been responsible for burning huge areas of forest containing valuable trees such as mahoganies, as well as many other forest products. In North America's temperate rain forests logging companies have been leaving a quarter of the wood lying on the ground.

SUBSIDISED DEFORESTATION

Logging in the temperate rain forests of the USA and Canada has been shown to be uneconomic and it has had to be supported by government subsidies. During the 1980s the North American Forestry Service spent around US $40 million of government (tax payers') money each year, in this way. This meant that American tax payers were paying millions of dollars to sell some of the world's largest and oldest trees to countries like Japan at a discounted price. At one stage the prices were so artificially low that 400 year old trees were being sold for less than the cost of a cheeseburger. In Britain, subsidies have also encouraged the felling of ancient woodlands and the establishment of large conifer plantations.

Valuable trees killed by flooding caused by the construction of the Samuel Dam in Brazil.

FORESTS AND THE MEAT INDUSTRY

At first glance it is not obvious to see why eating meat might be connected with forest destruction. But in Central America cattle ranching is thought to have caused the loss of two-thirds of the region's forests. Between 1975 and 1995, 90 per cent of the beef from animals raised on previously forested land went to the USA, mainly for use in hamburgers. The trade was encouraged because beef could be produced at between a quarter and half the cost of producing it in North America. Brazil is another country in which landowners have been subsidized by their government to cut down or burn forest to create cattle ranches – with disastrous effects.

There are other, less obvious, ways in which forests in developing countries are being destroyed because of the international meat industry. European Union (EU) agricultural policies are part of the problem. A good example is the demand by European countries for cheap pig food, supported by the EU. In Thailand this has led to the destruction of huge areas of tropical rain forest, in order to grow cassava. Cassava starch is turned into tapioca and this has become a major food for pigs. In Thailand cassava is grown as a cash crop by farmers mainly in the north-east of the country. The area under cultivation has increased from 100,000 ha in 1965 to more than a million hectares today because of the demand for pig food. The Netherlands alone imports around 40 million tonnes of tapioca each year. Deforestation of upland areas of Thailand has led to flash floods and hundreds of deaths each year during the 1990s.

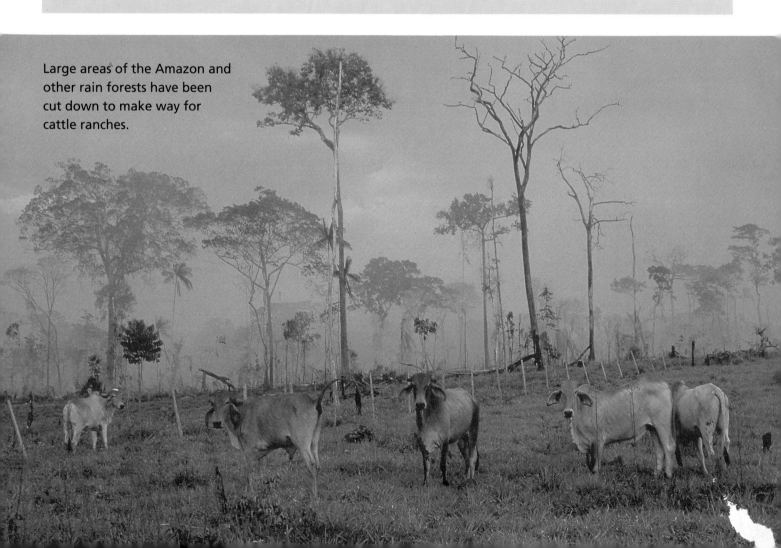

Large areas of the Amazon and other rain forests have been cut down to make way for cattle ranches.

Although commercial logging is not the only cause of deforestation, it has caused the degradation of vast areas of rain forest, and the roads built by the logging companies have opened up the forests enabling settlers to move in.

UNFAIR SHARES

Probably the largest cause of deforestation overall is the unequal distribution of wealth and power. The current world economic system encourages individuals and businesses to become as wealthy as they can in as short a time as possible. This means that the rules developed by local communities over very long periods of time in order to protect and manage their environments are now being broken. For example, powerful companies controlled only by a handful of people are able to cause enormous damage to forests and to push out local people, without really being challenged. But large numbers of poor people are also moving into rain forests and cutting down plots because they have been forced or obliged to move from other areas.

In Indonesia, an estimated one million families who have been relocated as part of the country's controversial transmigration scheme are each clearing half a hectare of new forest every year. This is because rain forest soils are generally too poor to support cultivation for more than a few years. When families do find good agricultural land they are often forced off by powerful land owners. This is particularly true in Brazil, where 4.5 per cent of the landowners own 81 per cent of all farmland and 70 per cent of rural families have no land at all.

▼ People moved from the over-crowded island of Sumatra to outlying islands, as part of the Indonesian government's transmigration scheme, have cut down rain forest to grow rice and other crops.

Many tropical countries now have enormous debts to institutions such as the World Bank, which lend money for 'development projects'. Because of their debts, these countries are under pressure to cut down their forests in order to try to make as much money as they can. This may be through selling the timber, constructing dams that will generate hydro-electric power or through plantation agriculture such as the cultivation of African oil palm (grown for oil which is used in many foods, soap and cosmetics). Foreign aid in the form of money or expertise from abroad which is given to less wealthy countries, has also led to forest loss. In some cases loans to developing countries, such as Guyana, have only been made on the understanding that foreign companies will be allowed to come and exploit the timber.

DISAPPEARING FORESTS IN SCANDINAVIA

Sweden and Finland are two countries that are thought by many to be models of good forest management. Sweden has 58 per cent of its land covered in forests whilst Finland has nearly 70 per cent. In both countries forest cover is rising. However, this has hidden the fact that a wildlife crisis has developed in Scandinavia.

An aerial view of a large African oil palm plantation and the workers' accommodation in south-west Cameroon.

In Finland only about 3 per cent of the ancient 'old-growth' forests remain. These forests are the last refuges of rare European plants, and animals such as moose, bear, lynx, wolves and wolverine. Until recently the forests on the mountains in northern Scandinavia remained relatively untouched. Now they are scheduled to be cut down. Foresters in both countries say, quite correctly, that several trees are planted for each one cut down. But the replacement forests typically consist of a single tree species, such as lodgepole pine or spruce, which cannot support the same variety of wildlife.

In Sweden it is not only plant and animal species that are facing extinction because of the destruction of the ancient forests: an ancient way of life is also under threat. The nomadic Saami, or Lapps, of Sweden have used the northern forests for centuries, spending the winters there with their herds of reindeer. The new plantation forests do not support the lichens that the reindeer need to eat to survive the winter. At the same time, some timber companies regard reindeer as pests and are trying to exclude the Saami by law.

For hundreds of years Saami people and their reindeer herds have relied on the wild forests in northern Scandinavia during the winter months.

THE FUEL-WOOD CRISIS

Throughout the world, more than 2 billion people rely on fuel wood for cooking or heating. As more trees are cut down, wood is becoming increasingly scarce across large parts of sub-Saharan Africa, the Middle East and Asia. Today more than 100 million people are unable to find enough fuel wood for even their most basic energy needs.

In many developing countries fuel-wood accounts for a large proportion of all energy consumption. More than 90 per cent of the energy used in countries such as Burkina Faso, Tanzania, Nepal, and Ethiopia comes from wood. Wood even provides oil-rich Nigeria with 80 per cent of its energy needs.

In the foothills of Nepal women now need to spend a day collecting the firewood that their mothers would have been able to collect in just one hour. Keeping home fires alight in parts of Nepal and Tanzania now takes 230 person days per family per year. Families in Ougadougou in Burkina Faso and Port au Prince in Haiti spend as much as 30 per cent of their income on fuelwood.

A young girl in Kathmandu, Nepal, carries a basket of firewood to market.

FOREST DEATH

Atmospheric pollution has been having a serious effect on forests in many parts of the world. In the early 1980s some European forests began to suffer from what came to be known as *Waldsterben,* which means 'forest death' in German. Germany was the first country to become affected, and more than half of the forests there are now suffering. Nearly half a million square kilometres of forests in 19 European countries are also dying. The problem, however, is not restricted to Europe: it is now affecting forests in 37 out of 50 US states, in China, and in nearly one million hectares of the former Soviet Union.

Scientists have identified more than 180 possible causes, ranging from errors in the way the trees were planted, to acid rain and climate change. It is now generally agreed that the cause is the combined effect of pollutants such as ozone from car exhausts and acid rain from the burning of fossil fuels.

When there is less wood for people to use, they begin to economize. Some families in developing nations no longer have enough wood to boil their drinking water, which means that they are more likely to catch water-borne diseases. In some areas people gather animal dung to burn as fuel, but this has the effect of removing what would otherwise have been an important source of fertilizer from the soil. Every year, Asians and Africans burn enough dung to grow 20 million tonnes of grain.

▼ Air pollution has been partly responsible for the death of forests near industrial areas. This is a scene from near Port Talbot in Wales.

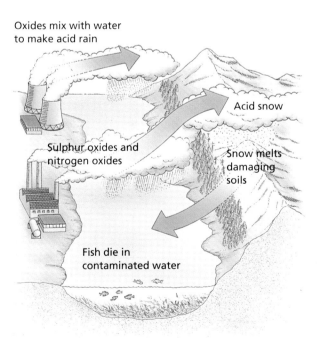

Oxides mix with water to make acid rain

Sulphur oxides and nitrogen oxides

Acid snow

Snow melts damaging soils

Fish die in contaminated water

WHAT IS BEING DONE?

Around the world many people are very concerned about what is happening to forests. Countless individuals, environmental groups and some governments are trying to find ways to protect and manage forests for the future.

There are many different issues involved in saving forests, and different actions are needed in different places. Where large-scale destructive logging is going on, major changes in attitude are needed now, from governments, international organizations and multinational companies. Unfortunately, many governments – such as those of Guyana, Guinea and the Solomon Islands – are still encouraging the logging of their forests because of the huge sums of money that they and the logging companies will make from selling the timber.

Mayan people in Belize protesting about the logging of rain forest by a multinational company in south Toledo.

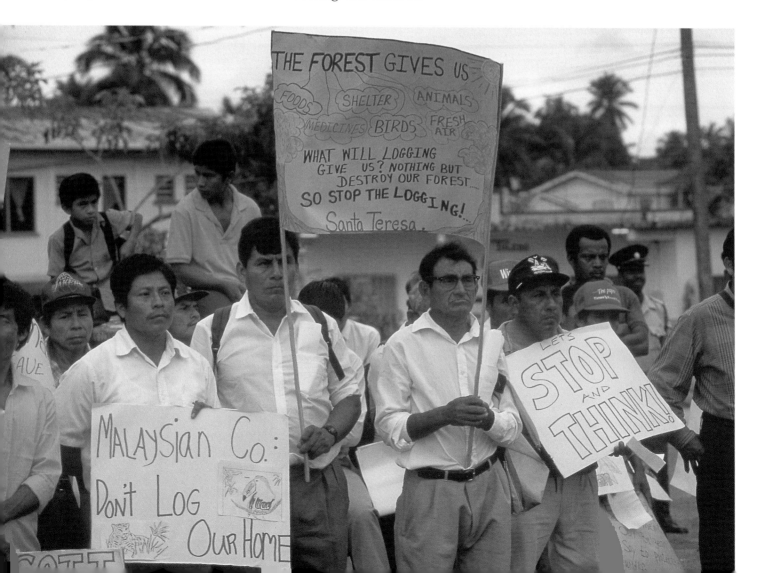

However, other governments, such as that of the UK, and some powerful organizations, like the World Bank, now accept that the rate of forest loss is a serious problem and that some of their policies and funding have led to an increase in forest destruction. Many conservationists believe that there should be a complete and immediate ban on the logging of all 'ancient growth' forests and suggest that this may even mean 'compensating' companies for not logging certain areas.

REFORESTING VIETNAM

The Vietnam War, which ended in 1975, left 22,000 square kilometres of forest destroyed or seriously damaged. In 1986, Vietnam began its National Conservation Strategy, which aims to regrow large areas of the country's forests. The plan is to plant at least 500 million trees a year in the hope that forest cover will return to about 50 per cent of the country. Tree planting has become one of the official activities of Vietnamese school children and every pupil must not only plant a tree but also look after it.

People planting new trees in north Vietnam in an effort to repair the damage caused during the Vietnam War and by excessive logging.

Background: New Zealand has some of the largest pine plantations in the world.
Inset: Christmas trees can be grown in an environmentally friendly way by using sheep to keep the weeds down instead of herbicides or pesticides. This plantation is in Denmark.

SUSTAINABLE FORESTS

The key issues of forest conservation revolve around sustainability – using forests and the animals and plants that live in them, in ways that do not permanently damage them. This means taking only as much timber or other products as the forests can support so that they will continue to be productive in future years. It also means respecting people who have traditional rights to forests.

Currently 95 per cent of all charcoal used in the UK is imported. The wood can come from anywhere, but is mainly from tropical forests, including the mangrove forests of Southeast Asia and the rain forests of South America. In Britain, however, there has been a long tradition of making charcoal from British wood which only began to die out 50 years ago.

Today, British forests are once again starting to produce charcoal, using the traditional, sustainable system of woodland management called coppicing. Many different sorts of trees are used, including ash, hazel, oak, sweet chestnut and hornbeam. In this system trees are cut to the ground, but new stems quickly grow back and are harvested at 15 year intervals. Harvesting the forest in this way provides a range of wildlife habitats, and encourages wild flowers and butterflies.

It has been calculated that Britain's broadleaved woodlands are growing about 2.4 million tonnes of hardwood each year, but only a third of this is harvested. Since it takes 6 tonnes of wood to make each tonne of charcoal, all the charcoal that Britain needs could be made by using just 15 per cent of what is currently going to waste.

The wealthy countries of the world must try and reduce their consumption of forest products in general, and increase the use of recycled materials such as paper and board. In the USA more than half of all the paper used is used for packaging and it is estimated that in under 50 years 3 billion trees will be needed each year, just to wipe the bottoms of the world's population.

The use of more wood from plantations will help save ancient forests and also the millions of species of plants and animals that live in them. Many forest species are now threatened with extinction, and environmental groups are pressing for bans on the national and international trade in them.

Hundreds of different products are now made out of recycled paper. These include newspapers, packaging and envelopes.

PROTECTED AREAS

Like the animals that live in them, only a tiny proportion of the world's remaining forests have any legal protection. Environmental organizations such as the World Wide Fund for Nature (WWF) and Friends of the Earth are trying to help save forests by campaigning for their urgent protection. They are also helping to inform governments and the public about the rates of destruction and possible effects of forest loss. WWF has called for the setting up of more protected areas and is campaigning for 10 per cent of the world's forests to be protected by the year 2000.

People protesting to protect an area of rain forest in Hawaii.

For millions of indigenous people, sustainable forest use has been central to their cultures for thousands of years and it is no accident that many of the surviving areas of intact forest are or were until recently their homes. Traditional forest peoples want their rights to their lands guaranteed so that they can manage areas in their own ways. They do not want their traditional lands turned into parks from which they may then be excluded, or to be told by others how to manage their affairs.

NEW OPPORTUNITIES IN LATVIA

Latvia is one of the Baltic countries that used to be part of the Soviet Union. Nearly half the country is forested and timber is its main export. At present logging companies are clear-felling Latvian forests – under strict orders from the State Forestry Service. Most of the companies would prefer to leave dead and over-aged trees to provide habitats for owls, woodpeckers and insects. They would rather leave the forests in swampy areas – that have little timber value – to beavers and other wildlife. They know that clearing all the small trees, as they are obliged to do under Latvian law, actually costs them money.

Things are beginning to change. In the 15,000-hectare territory of Melzole, a forestry project has been set up in which the normal forestry rules don't apply. Foresters are not being forced to cut down every tree, and wildlife and trees have benefited. In one 4.5-hectare plot there has been an estimated saving of over US $1,000 by leaving some trees standing.

If the Latvian government encourages all the timber companies to work in this more environmentally sensitive, and more cost-effective, way the future will be brighter for the forests, for wildlife such as wolves, elk and black stork, and for the foresters themselves.

Nearly half of Latvia is forested but timber companies have the capacity to clear fell most of Latvia in 10–20 years, if the forests are not managed sustainably.

A Mexican child reads about World Environment Day at a school in a remote village surrounded by mangrove forest in the Yucatan Peninsula.

A ROLE FOR EVERYONE

In summary, there are a number of important ways of conserving forests and the most important of these are: action by governments, multinational organizations and companies to ban uncontrolled logging; the sustainable use of forests; reducing our consumption of forest products in general; increasing the use of plantation products and recycled materials; respecting the rights of indigenous peoples; creating properly protected areas; introducing and enforcing bans on the trade in rare species; and reducing air pollution.

Individuals can also help to slow down forest loss by using more recycled things – paper, toilet paper and kitchen towel, for example – and by buying eco-labelled products (see box on facing page) wherever possible. We can also help by trying to pollute the environment less – for example by not using the car so often and trying to make journeys by public transport – and by planting trees locally.

ECO-LABELLING

At present it is not clear where much of the wood we use has come from, or whether a door or toilet seat is made from a tree that was illegally felled. The idea behind eco-labelling is to enable people to see where the wood products we use have come from. Under this scheme, all products that come from well-managed forests will carry a label to show this. This will enable people to choose which to buy and so help support the sustainable use of forests.

The Forest Stewardship Council (FSC) was set up in 1993 to provide a way of checking where timber comes from and how it has been harvested. Under the scheme, forests around the world are visited and assessed. If they are producing timber in a way that is sustainable for the forseeable future and meet other social and environmental criteria, they become 'certified' and receive the FSC stamp of approval. To meet the FSC standard, forests must be managed to make sure that:

A Mexican man holds up a sawn plank from a forest that has recently been certified. This means the local people have a plan to cut timber and protect the forest for the future.

- The harvest of all products (whether timber or products such as nuts or fibres) can be sustained, that soils and water will be protected, and that the forest's contribution to local weather and global climate patterns remains unchanged.

- The original variety of plants, animals and other organisms depending on the forest can be maintained.

- Indigenous people, forestry employees and local communities must benefit, as well as the local and national economies.

- A number of forests have already been certified in the UK, Papua New Guinea, the USA, Poland, South Africa, Zimbabwe and Mexico. When products from these forests go on sale they display the FSC logo and the consumer can be assured that they are helping to ensure the long term future of forests.

The FSC logo is used to enable people to choose products made from wood that has come from well-managed forests.

WHAT CAN WE DO?

The scale of deforestation is so great that many people think there is little they can do to help save our forests. Yet, ordinary people working together can be very powerful. While politicians and governments tend to think only a few years ahead, public opinion is often more far-sighted. Many people are worried about the effects of deforestation on future generations. In the past, public opinion has helped to change the law on hunting whales, on the protection of Antarctica and on lead in petrol. So what people think – and do – can have a real effect on how the world's forests are used.

A cubscout in the USA gathering old newspapers for recycling.

THINGS YOU CAN DO

● Become aware of the issues concerning the use of forests.

● Encourage your school, office and parents to use more recycled and 'certified' products using the FSC logo.

● Try to consume less. For example, you might avoid buying products with excessive packaging.

● Try to pollute the environment less. One way to do this is to use cars less and bicycles and public transport more. Air pollution kills forests and contributes to global warming.

● Join an environmental group, such as WWF or Friends of the Earth.

● Find out about tree-planting schemes in your area, and take part.

● Write to your government representative and ask what his or her party's policy is on forests, recycling and the FSC – and tell him or her what you think about these issues.

The use of public transport in countries like Denmark helps reduce the atmospheric pollution that is killing European forests.

A volunteer in Australia planting and watering a tree seedling.

PUBLIC OPINION AND THE WORLD BANK

The World Bank lends large sums of money to governments for development projects around the world. However, it has often faced strong criticism because of the severe environmental and social effects of some of the projects it has funded. In one case, the World Bank loaned money to Ivory Coast and Ghana in Africa to open up their last remaining natural forest to large-scale logging. However, the Bank did not ask for guarantees that the forest would be managed sustainably.

Because of this, WWF and Friends of the Earth organized a card-writing campaign in the UK to try to change the World Bank's forest policy. Over 30,000 cards were sent to Members of Parliament. As a result of this, and similar campaigns in other countries, the World Bank was forced to adopt a new policy stating that it 'will under no circumstances finance commercial logging in primary tropical moist forests.'

FORESTS FOR THE FUTURE

The world's forests are disappearing fast, especially in the tropics. If current trends continue, in 50 years only small patches of tropical rain forest will survive and most of the world's remaining forests will be in the temperate and boreal regions of North America, Scandinavia and Siberia. Some scientists fear that we are on the brink of a global environmental catastrophe. It's almost too late, but there is just time if action is taken quickly.

Temperate forest still covers much of the French and Spanish Pyrenees and is protected within national parks.

As we have seen, there are many things that can be done by us as individuals, by our governments and by large companies to save the world's forests. The responsibility for stopping large-scale destruction lies mainly with the governments and citizens of the rich nations. It is the demand for forest products for non-essential uses such as excessive packaging that has helped destroy many forests. As individuals we can consume less, recycle more, buy goods from sustainably managed forests, join environmental pressure groups and campaign for our governments and businesses to act more responsibly. Governments and international organizations must take action to protect areas of natural 'old growth' forest throughout the world. This may include signing international agreements prohibiting the trade in tree species that are near extinction and in wood that does not come from properly managed forests.

Protecting forests is not just a question of money. In 1990 representatives of the seven wealthiest nations, known as the G7, reached an agreement to pledge up to US $500 million to combat the destruction of the Amazon rain forest. The latest satellite information from Brazil, in 1996, has shown that the rate of destruction has increased by 34 per cent since 1992. What is needed is a fundamental change in the lifestyles of the people of the rich nations. Some people may object to this but it is a small price to pay to protect the future of the forests – and the planet.

At present it is the people in the developing nations – who rely on forests for their immediate needs – who are losing out. For them it is not a question of paying more for products or using less paper, it is a matter of life or death.

The challenge is to protect the world's forests in ways that keep the planet's life-support system in working order while continuing to satisfy the basic human needs for housing, warmth, clean water and fresh air. This is not an easy task, but if governments, individuals and environmental groups work towards a common goal of halting and reversing the loss and degradation of all types of woodland then the outlook for the twenty-first century will be brighter.

Prospectors and mining companies have caused destruction of large areas of the Amazon rain forests. In many cases the rain forest trees are cut down to make charcoal to smelt the metal ores.

GLOSSARY

AROMATIC PLANTS Plants that contain substances with strong aromas (smells), often used to make perfumes.

BOREAL Northern.

CONIFER An evergreen tree which usually has cones.

CONSERVATIONIST A person who believes that nature should be protected.

COPPICING A forestry system where trees are cut in such a way that new poles grow from the stumps and are harvested every 15–20 years.

CANOPY The uppermost layer of branches formed by a tree or trees.

DECIDUOUS FOREST A forest containing trees that shed their leaves each year.

DEFORESTATION The removal of trees from an area.

ECO-LABEL A label providing information about where a particular product has come from and relevant environmental details.

ECOSYSTEM A community of animals and plants and the environment they live in.

EVERGREEN A description of trees that keep their leaves all year round. The opposite of deciduous.

FLOODED FOREST An area of forest which is flooded permanently or at certain times of the year.

GLOBAL WARMING The gradual warming up of the surface of the planet as a result of a change in the composition of atmospheric gases, especially an increase in the percentage of carbon dioxide.

HABITAT The natural home of a particular plant or animal.

INDIGENOUS Belonging originally or naturally to a particular place.

LATEX A milky sap that is produced by various plants and trees.

MANGROVE FOREST Evergreen forest found along some tropical coastlines. The trees have special roots that stick up from the mud and can take in oxygen.

MONTANE FOREST Forest which occurs above 900 m.

MULTINATIONAL COMPANIES Large companies that operate on a global scale.

NON-TIMBER FOREST PRODUCTS These are products, other than timber, which are harvested from forests. Examples include fruits, latexes, nuts and medicines.

NOMADIC Describes people who do not have any one home location but move regularly from place to place.

PLANTATION An area in which a single crop is planted, often in rows.

RAIN FOREST A forest that has high rainfall all year round.

RECYCLED MATERIAL Materials that are made from waste. For example, paper made from waste paper.

SUSTAINABLE A way of using resources that does not threaten their long-term survival or the survival of the plants and animals, including humans, which depend upon them.

TEMPERATE Mild or moderate.

TRANSMIGRATION The relocation of often tens of thousands of people from their homeland to another location.

TROPICS The area characterized by high temperatures and rainfall that lies between the Tropics of Capricorn and Cancer.

FURTHER INFORMATION

ADDRESSES TO WRITE TO

Friends of the Earth
26–28 Underwood Street
London N1 7JQ
Tel: 0171 490 1555

Reforest the Earth
48 Bethel Street
Norwich
Norfolk NR2 1NR
Tel: 01603 631007

The Living Earth Foundation
Warwick House
106 Harrow Road
London W2 1XD
Tel: 0171 2581823

The World Rainforest Movement
Chapel Row
Chadlington
Oxfordshire OX7 3NA
Tel: 01608 676691

World Wide Fund for Nature
Panda House
Weyside Park
Catteshall Lane
Godalming
Surrey GU7 1XR
Tel: 01483 426444

Survival International
11–15 Emerald Street
London WC1N 3QL
Tel: 0171 242 1441

Forest Stewardship Council
Unit D, Station Building
Llanidloes
Powys SY18 6EB
Tel: 01686 413916

BOOKS TO READ

The Tree Book by Edward Milner (Collins and Brown, 1992)

The Good Wood Guide (Friends of the Earth)

The Wayland Atlas of Rain Forests by Anna Lewington (Wayland, 1996)

The Last Rain Forests ed. Mark Collins (Mitchell Beazley, 1990)

The Conservation Atlas of Tropical Forests: Africa ed. Jeffrey Sayer, Caroline Harcourt and Mark Collins (Macmillan in association with IUCN, 1992)

The Conservation Atlas of Tropical Forests: Asia & The Pacific ed. Mark Collins, Jeffrey Sayer and Timothy Whitmore (Macmillan in association with IUCN, 1991)

The Rainforests: A Celebration ed. Lisa Silcock (Barrie & Jenkins, 1989)

Jungle by Theresa Greenaway (Dorling Kindersley, 1994)

Discovering the Amazon (Reader's Digest, 1994)

Amazon: The Flooded Forest by Michael Goulding (BBC Books, 1989)

The Mighty Rainforest by John Nicol (David & Charles, 1990)

Poisoned Arrows by George Monbiot (Abacus, 1989)

Baka: People of the Rainforest by Lisa Silcock (Channel 4 Television, 1988)

Rainforest Amerindians by Anna Lewington (Wayland, 1992)

In Papua New Guinea by Christina Dodwell (Pan Books Ltd, 1983)

MULTI-MEDIA EDUCATION PACKS

The Decade of Destruction (World Wide Fund for Nature, 1986/Central Independent Television, 1991)

Land Habitats (Wayland Multimedia, 1997)

FILMS AND VIDEOS

The Decade of Destruction by Adrian Cowell (Central Independent Television)

The Flooded Forest by Michael Goulding (BBC Video)

Vietnam: After The Fire by Edward Milner (Acacia Productions)

Last Tree in Thailand by Edward Milner (Acacia Productions)

Baka: People of the Rainforest by Phil Agland (DJA River Films for Channel 4)

The Emerald Forest (Embassy Pictures, 1985)

The Mission (Goldcrest Films, 1985)

Gorillas in the Mist (Warner Bros, 1988)

Medicine Man (Cinergi, 1992)

Nomads of the Wind (BBC Video)

Spirit of Trees (Channel 4 Video)

INDEX

PICTURE ACKNOWLEDGEMENTS

Bruce Coleman Collection 9 (Luiz Claudio Marigo), 15 (Konrad Wothe), 22 top (Alain Compost); Bryan and Cherry Alexander 18 (Edward Parker), 31; Forlaget Flachs 36 inset (Ole Steen Hansen), 37 (Dieter Betz), 43 (Svend Erik Andersen); Hedgehog House 16 (Colin Monteath), 36 (Lynda Harper); Oxford Scientific Films 24 (Martyn Colbeck), 43 (Bob Goodale); Edward Parker 39, 40, 41; Science Photo Library cover background (NASA), 8 (Simon Fraser), 14 (Dr Morley Read), 22 bottom (Philippe Plailly/Eurelios), 33 (Simon Fraser); Still Pictures 4 (Alain Compost), 10 (Nigel Dickinson), 11 (Mark Edwards), 13 (Bojan Brecelj), 17 right (Dario Novellino), 19 (Mark Edwards), 20 (Mark Edwards), 21 (Mark Edwards), 23 (Mark Edwards), 25 (Jonathan Kaplan), 27 (John Maier), 28 (Mark Edwards), 29 (Paul Harrison), 30 (Edward Parker), 32 (Jørgen Schytte), 34 (Nigel Dickinson), 35 (Heldur Netocny), 44 (Georges Lopez), 45 (Mark Edwards); Tony Stone Images 5 (Vince Streano), 6 (Brett Baunton), 12 (Daniel J Cox), 26 (Zigy Kalunzy), 38 (G Brad Lewis), 42 (Bruce Forster); Wayland Picture Library 17 left; Zefa front cover.
All artwork is by Peter Bull, except the book icons used on page 2, the contents page and chapter headings, which are by Tina Barber.